Fantastic Creatures

Andrew Whitmore

B   ITZ
N   IN
E   TION

HORWITZ
MARTIN
EDUCATION

Horwitz Martin Education
A Division of Horwitz Publications Pty Ltd
55 Chandos St
St Leonards NSW 2065
Australia

Horwitz Martin Education
Unit 15, Cressex Enterprise Centre
Lincoln Road
High Wycombe, Bucks HP12 3RL
United Kingdom

a black dog book
Designed by Josie Semmler
Cover photograph by John Brash. Digital composition by Josie Semmler.
Illustrations by Peter Gouldthorpe pp. 5, 6, 20, 21, 33, 36, 51, 52, 67, 71, 73.
Printed and bound in Australia by Hyde Park Press.

National Library of Australia
Cataloguing information
Whitmore, Andrew, 1955–.
  Fantastic creatures

  Bibliography.
  Includes index.
  ISBN 0 7253 1945 3.

Thoth
The Egyptian
god of wisdom,
mathematics and writing.

1. Animals - Juvenile literature. 2. Animals - Juvenile fiction. 3. Animals,
Mythical - Juvenile literature. 4. Animals, Mythical - Juvenile fiction.
5. Monsters - Juvenile fiction. 6. Monsters - Juvenile literature. I. Title.
(Series: Phenomena II).

001.944

The publishers would like to thank P. Millard for permission to reproduce
the photograph on p. 82. Other images are from the editor's, author's and
designer's collections or are in the public domain. Every effort has been
made to contact original sources, where known, for permissions. If an
infringement has inadvertently occurred, the editor wishes to apologise.
The publisher and the editor would like to thank Garry Chapman and
Vicki Hazell, the educational consultants on this series.

1 2 3 4
00 01 02

Contents

Introduction   **1**

Chapter 1   **Tall stories**   **3**

Chapter 2   **How to build a monster**   **18**

Chapter 3   **Mistaken identity**   **33**

Chapter 4   **Living proof**   **50**

Chapter 5   **Lost worlds**   **71**

Where to from here?   **89**

Andrew's note   **91**

Index   **92**

Introduction

NOBODY HAS ever seen a dragon, but everyone knows what they look like. In fact, some of the most famous animals in the world cannot be found in any zoo. Is there really a monster living in Scotland's Loch Ness? Do wild ape-men really roam the forests of North America, leaving 40 cm (1 ft 3 inch) footprints in the snow? Or are they just figments of the imagination?

Stories about weird and wonderful creatures are as old as humanity itself. Birds big enough to carry grown elephants in their claws. Giants the size of mountains. Glamorous mermaids and hairy ogres. Dragons and sea-monsters and dogs with three heads. The ancient world was a frightening place, and it's easy to see how people could have imagined all kinds of monsters lurking

Dragons are mythical creatures, usually represented as huge winged reptiles.

just out of sight, waiting to pounce on them the very moment their backs were turned.

No doubt a lot of the tales about such creatures were completely made up. People have always liked to swap scary stories around the campfire. Stories would have become exaggerated over the years. Others might have been based on second-hand reports of foreign animals. Imagine what the original white settlers in Australia thought when they first saw a kangaroo!

So, what exactly are these fabulous creatures that have fascinated so many people all over the world for so many thousands of years? Is there a chance any of them might really exist? Or, deep down, do we just wish they did?

chapter 1
Tall stories

Imagine...

"TELL US a story, Grandfather."
Ina and her family squatted around
the fire, plucking juicy pieces of baked
fish from the coals.

"Yes, Grandfather," Rewa said. "Tell us
a story about the old days."

Their grandfather laughed. He had
even fewer teeth than baby Muhu, and
his face was as brown and wrinkled as
dry seaweed.

"What kind of story?" he said.

"Tell us about the Giant with Teeth of
Fire," Rewa said.

Ina nodded. Both she and Rewa had
heard the tale many times before, but it
was still one of their favourites. And,
somehow, their grandfather never told a
story the same way twice.

"The Giant with Teeth of Fire, eh?" Grandfather sat back on his haunches. "He was one mean fellow, that one. Taller than ten palm trees and so heavy that the whole island shook whenever he stamped his foot."

"Ten palm trees, Grandfather?" Ina asked. She could have sworn it had been only eight last time he'd told the story.

"Oh, yes, little one. At the very least. And his teeth, they burned like coals of fire. His breath was so hot it singed the leaves on trees for miles around every time he opened his mouth. And when he smiled—ah, it was terrifying to see, believe me. The glare of his burning teeth was brighter than the sun!

"He lived right up there." Grandfather pointed at the dark bulk of the mountain behind them. "In a big cave. Most of the time he just slept. And a good thing, too. Otherwise he would have burnt up the whole island. But, now and then, he would wake up and come striding down the mountain, smoke and fire pouring from his mouth as he bared his terrible teeth. What a fearsome sight! All the villagers would run and hide whenever they saw him coming!

"Now, some of the young men of the village thought how wonderful it would be if they could steal some of the giant's fire for themselves. Because no one knew how to make fire in those days, you see. They had to eat all their food raw and had nothing to keep them warm in the chill of the night.

"So, one day, the bravest and most daring of the young men got together and gathered bundles of dried palm leaves. Then they quietly made their way up to the giant's cave.

"Luckily, the giant was fast asleep. With every breath, tongues of flame bubbled out through his huge lips, lighting up the whole cave.

"The brave young men crept closer and closer. If the giant woke up, he would surely kill them all. At last, they were close enough to poke the bundles of dried leaves into the little flames dancing around the giant's mouth. They waited for the leaves to catch fire, then quickly turned and raced back down the mountain.

"And that," Grandfather said with a smile, "is why we now have delicious feasts like this." He glanced at the piece of baked fish he was holding, then opened his mouth and popped it in.

"But that's not the end," Rewa protested. "Tell us the rest. You know, how the giant wakes up and chases them down the mountain. And how they hide in a cave. And how the giant tries to trick them into coming out. And—"

Grandfather laughed. "Ah," he said, turning towards Rewa with a mischievous gleam in his eye. "That's another story."

THE END

No ONE KNOWS who made up the story of the Giant with Teeth of Fire. It has been told and re-told for countless generations throughout the Fiji islands. Perhaps it was based on half-forgotten memories of volcanic eruptions. What better way to explain the smoke and flames spewing out of a volcano than by blaming it on some fire-breathing giant who lived inside the mountain? And what else could possibly have caused the very ground to shake except a giant's mighty footsteps?

But there has to be more to it than that. Stories about giants are found throughout the whole world. According to legend, they were once so common in England that a boy named Jack spent half his life killing them. Ancient Jewish writings tell of giants who were 3.5 km (2 miles) tall. There are Greek giants, African giants, Australian giants. There are two Central American giants who amused themselves by piling up mountains, then knocking them down with earthquakes. The Maoris of New Zealand tell how their entire country was pulled up from the bottom of the sea by a giant fisherman.

In the fairytale, Jack and the Beanstalk, Jack's bean plant leads him to a fantastic world in the sky where he finds giants and castles and geese that lay golden eggs!

In fact, no matter where or when people lived, they all seem to have believed in the existence of giants at some time or another.

The only question is why?

Real-life giants

There really are giants, of course. You've probably seen them on television hundreds of times. You might even have met some of them in person, or got their autograph. Perhaps you will even grow up to be one yourself.

Technically, any male human over 2 metres (6 ft 6 inches) tall is classified as a giant. The same thing goes for women over 187 cm (6 ft 1 inch) in height. That makes Shaquille O'Neal a giant, along with many other basketball players.

The average height of an adult man is 173 cm (5 ft 8 inches). The average height of an NBA basketball player is 201 cm (6 ft 7 inches).

The tallest human being, whose height we can be certain of, was Robert Wadlow. Born in Illinois, USA, in 1918, he grew to be over 305 cm (10 ft) tall and weighed 200 kg (440 lb). As far as anyone knows, however, he didn't have burning teeth—and neither does Shaquille O'Neal. Nor would either of them have been able to wade knee-deep in the ocean the way the legendary King Og of Bashan was said to have done during Noah's flood.

Legendary giants—the kind you read about in stories—aren't simply a bit taller than the average person, they are absolutely huge! And the odds of you ever seeing one of them is pretty slim. There is no evidence that creatures like this ever existed and, according to the laws of science, they cannot exist.

Too big to be true?

An average human being stands about 173 cm (5 ft 8 inches) tall and weighs around 60 kg (132 lb). For someone to be double that size, they would have to weigh four times as much. Double that again, and their weight would be sixteen times greater. Someone as tall as a two-storey building would weigh 7 tonnes!

An African elephant weighs up to 7 tonnes. It needs four legs to carry the weight.

This is physically impossible. Even bodies the size of Robert Wadlow's have difficulty working properly. Wadlow could only walk with the aid of a stick and had to wear braces on his ankles to stop them collapsing under his own weight. It was so hard for his heart to pump blood from one end of his body to the other that he had virtually no feeling in his feet at all.

In fact, this was what killed him. One of the braces wasn't fitted properly. But Wadlow didn't notice anything until his skin became badly blistered. An infection set in, and he quickly died of blood poisoning. He was only 22 years old.

Giants of old

This statue of Robert Wadlow in his home town of Alton shows just how tall he was.

If it's impossible for giants to exist, why is it that so many people in so many different countries thought that they did?

One reason is that people living long ago had a very different way of looking at the world than we do. Nowadays, most of us believe that science and technology are constantly improving. If you're buying a car, for example, you'd probably choose the most recent model you could afford, rather than one several years old. The same goes for computers, household gadgets, video games and just about everything else you can think of. And we expect that most things will just keep on getting better and better in the future as technology improves.

In the past, however, people often thought the exact opposite. As far as they were concerned, everything was just getting worse and worse. They imagined that their ancestors were a lot stronger, braver and smarter than they were, with powers and abilities beyond their wildest dreams. This may seem strange to us, but they had good reasons for thinking that way. For one thing, it was very often true.

Dreams of a golden age

Throughout history, civilisations have come and gone. Some have been wiped out by natural disasters, or torn apart by civil war, or overrun by invaders. The period that followed was often a "Dark Age" of ignorance and poverty. Apart from muddled stories handed down from one generation to the next, almost everything these civilisations had achieved was completely forgotten.

Not all of them, however, vanished without a trace. Many left behind ruined cities and temples. These were often built on such a massive scale that people

11

assumed they were the cities of giants.
Imagine how a desert tribesman in Egypt
felt when he saw the Great Pyramid at
Giza or the 20 metre (65 ft) tall statues of
a pharaoh and his wife carved on the side
of a mountain at Abu Simbel.

The Great Pyramid at Giza
is the largest Egyptian
pyramid. It is 140 metres
(459 ft) high and is built
from granite blocks each
weighing 2.5 tonnes.

Besides, since these long-
lost ancestors had obviously
been so superior to them in
every other way, didn't it
stand to reason they must
have been much bigger as
well?

Giant builders

Traces of giants' handiwork seemed to be
everywhere. Ancient Greeks believed that
one-eyed giants, called Cyclopses, built
the mighty fortresses whose remains they
found at places like Mycenae and Tiryns.
The great stone circles dotted throughout
Britain and Ireland were also once
thought to be the work of giants. The
most famous of these, Stonehenge, is
known locally as The Giant's Dance.

It wasn't just ancient buildings and
monuments that seemed to be the work
of giants. They were also thought to be

responsible for many natural features.

The Giant's Causeway on the north coast of County Antrim in Northern Ireland is one of the region's biggest tourist attractions. Although actually formed by a volcanic eruption tens of thousands of years ago, the 40,000 or so cube-shaped lumps of rock were said to be the remains of a gigantic roadway that had once stretched all the way to Scotland.

Some parts of the landscape were actually thought to be giants—or what was left of them anyway. According to Greek mythology, for example, the Atlas Mountains in North-West Africa were the petrified remains of a giant whose job it had been to hold the earth and sky apart.

> **petrify:**
> *to turn into stone.*

Giant bones

If anyone needed further proof that giants indeed existed, they only had to look at the monstrous skeletons that kept turning up from time to time. We now know these were actually the fossil remains of prehistoric animals like mammoths and cave bears. Since no one knew anything about these creatures back then, it isn't surprising they were mistaken for giants,

Mammoth fossil.

dragons and other fabulous creatures.

On the Mediterranean island of Sicily, for example, huge skulls were found with a single hole just under the forehead. These were thought to be the remains of gigantic one-eyed men and helped give rise to the legend of the Cyclopses. In fact, they were elephant skulls, the hole being where blood vessels and air passages ran down into the trunk.

species:

a particular group of living things.

It wasn't just the ancient Greeks who made this kind of mistake. A surgeon who examined bones found in France in 1613 declared them to be the skeleton of a giant with shoulders 2.5 metres (8 ft 2 inches) wide and eyes as big as dinner plates. Two hundred years later, they were identified as belonging to an early species of elephant.

If the bones obviously weren't anything like those of a human being, they were usually attributed to dragons. The people of Klagenfurt in Austria certainly had no doubts what the giant skull they discovered in the 16th century belonged to. They even built a large statue of a dragon in their town square to mark the occasion. But they were wrong.

The woolly rhinoceros is the prehistoric ancestor of the present rhinoceros.

In fact, the skull was that of a woolly rhinoceros.

Larger than life?

People throughout history have always loved a good story. And, just like a fisherman describing "the one that got away", ancient storytellers often made exaggerated claims about the heroes and villains of their tales.

The story of David and Goliath wouldn't be nearly as exciting if they had both been roughly the same size. We all love to see an underdog triumphing against the odds. Was Goliath really around three and a half metres (eleven and a half feet) tall? Probably not. But describing him that way certainly makes David's victory seem even more remarkable.

Later generations often exaggerated the size of their heroes as well. Charlemagne, who united the tribes living in the area we now call France and became their first king, was without doubt a remarkable man. At the time of his death in A.D. 814, he ruled most of Western Europe and had been married nine times. He was probably big and strong as well. Kings had to be in those days. But there's no reason to believe he was 2.4 metres (7 ft 10 inches) tall, or able to bend three horseshoes in his hands at once, the way legends claimed. But because he was so great in so many other ways, people tended to think he must have been great in size as well.

Stretching the truth

Not all stories concerning giants were meant to be taken seriously. A good example are the tales told about a gigantic American lumberjack named Paul Bunyan.

Even as a young boy, Paul was supposed to have been so big that every time he sneezed or coughed he blew the roofs off the neighbours' houses. When he jumped into the water at the beach, he made a splash so big it flooded the land for miles around.

Paul grew up to become the greatest timber-cutter who had ever lived. He chopped down trees so quickly his axe grew red-hot. Where other loggers kept dogs as pets, he had a giant blue ox called

Babe. One summer, when a twisty road prevented him from harvesting a particular group of trees, Paul is said to have hitched Babe to one end of it and pulled the road straight!

Of course, none of the people who told stories about Paul Bunyan believed he actually existed. If someone that big had been wandering around the United States a hundred years ago, he would hardly have gone unnoticed. They were just having a bit of fun. And the more exaggerated the stories were, the more their listeners enjoyed them.

Perhaps some of the tales about legendary giants of the past developed in much the same way.

No doubt there were people the size of Shaquille O'Neal in ancient times. There were probably even some as tall as Robert Wadlow. But there were no giants with teeth of fire or 20 metre (65 ft) high monsters like the one whose bones were reportedly dug up on the island of Crete during the days of the Roman Empire.

Human beings simply can't grow that big—except in people's imaginations.

> According to Scandinavian mythology, the whole world was made from the dead body of a giant named Ymir.

17

chapter 2
How to build a Monster

Imagine...

"HEY," HILARY SAID. "Look at this." Picking her way through a jumble of boxes and suitcases, Monica eventually found her sister hunched over a large, battered trunk. It had been raining all weekend, and they'd decided now was the perfect time to finally explore the attic of their new house—especially since the television still wasn't working properly. So far, all they'd found were a few clothes and some bundles of old newspapers.

"What is it?" Monica asked.

Hilary held up a dusty, leather bound book. "I don't know," she said, slowly flicking through the pages. "Seems to be some kind of diary. Kind of hard to read though. Must be really old. I wonder…" Suddenly, her grip on the book tightened. "Hey!" she said. "Listen to this!

The creature is getting bolder. Last night I could hear it slithering around near the cellar door. I'm too afraid to go down there any more, even in daylight. I have nailed the door shut as best I can and just pray it is strong enough to keep the thing from escaping…

Monica laughed. "Nice try, Hilary," she said. "But the old 'thing in the cellar' routine is a bit lame, don't you think?"

"I'm not making this up," Hilary told her. "Honest! Take a look for yourself if you don't believe me."

Monica grabbed the book and scanned the page her sister had been reading. Hilary was right about the handwriting. It was so jerky Monica could barely recognise some of the words at all. But enough of it made sense for her to realise Hilary was telling the truth.

"Wow!" she said. "Sounds just like one of those horror stories, doesn't it? Although I guess it was probably only rats or something."

"More like a snake," Hilary said. "It

slithered, remember. See if there's any more about it later on."

Most of the remaining pages, however, were almost completely unreadable. Something seemed to have been spilt over them and smeared the ink. One bit Monica could make out complained that the police *...found nothing whatsoever during the course of their investigations. They are apparently of the opinion that I am merely the victim of a recurring nightmare and advised me to drink a cup of hot milk each evening before retiring!*

Only the very last pages were undamaged. The writing here was even more untidy, as if it had been scribbled down in a hurry. As Monica read it, she felt her skin prickle with goose flesh.

My candle is burning low. Soon I will be in darkness. And then the beast will come.

It is outside now: waiting, lurking. I can hear it slapping against the door like a

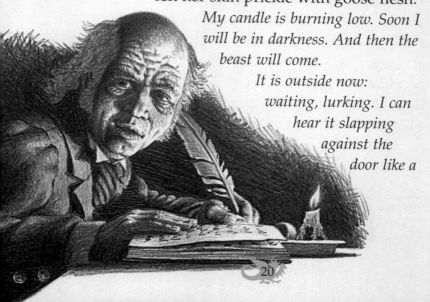

bundle of wet rope. The lock can't hold much longer. My blood runs cold to think what foul, misshapen brute will be revealed when the door finally opens.

I should have fled when I had the chance. Now it is too late. I will die here, devoured by a hell-spawned monster no one other than myself ever believed existed.

The door is starting to splinter! Something is pushing its way inside! Snaking towards me! Searching. Hunting.

Oh, my God! It…

"Keep going," Hilary said in a hushed voice. "What happened next?"

"That's all there is," Monica told her. "The writing just trails off. Almost as if…"

Hilary's face was as white as a sheet. "As if what?" she whispered.

"Well, as if something grabbed his arm." Monica glanced nervously over her shoulder. Suddenly it seemed awfully quiet and lonely in the attic. "You know, before he could finish the sentence."

THE END

A LOT OF HORROR stories end this way. That's because it's very hard to picture what a monster might actually look like. Even famous horror writers like H.P. Lovecraft have had trouble inventing truly frightening monsters. One critic complained that Lovecraft's monsters always turned out to be some kind of invisible, whistling octopus.

If you were asked to draw a monster, you would most likely find it impossible to imagine something that doesn't look in some way like an existing creature. Probably, the best you could do would be to borrow bits and pieces from the scariest animals you could find and put them all together. It might have the head of a snake, teeth like a shark and the body of a giant spider. Or you might give it six eyes and long blue tentacles.

When storytellers in ancient times wanted to invent a horrifying monster for their heroes to fight, they tended to do much the same thing.

How ugly can you get?

Monsters don't come much worse than the Gorgons. In Greek legends, these hideous women had snakes for hair, huge bulging eyes, bronze claws and tusks like a wild pig. Just to top it off, their skin was covered with scales. They were so horrible that anyone who looked at them was turned to stone. The hero Perseus solved this problem by using his polished shield as a mirror so he only ever saw their reflection. This way he was able to cut the head off one of them and use it as a weapon against his enemies.

There were three Gorgons—Medusa the Queen, Stheno the Mighty and Euryale the Far-Springer.

Harpies wouldn't have won too many beauty contests either. They had the body of a bird and the head and shoulders of a withered, half-starved woman. As well as being unpleasant to look at, they were also extremely dirty and smelly. Anything that came in contact with them was immediately polluted by their stink.

Mix and match

Taking part of one animal and sticking it on another has always been a popular way of creating monsters. The ancient Greeks did it all the time.

Griffins had the head of an eagle and the body of a lion. (Some, known as hippogriffs, had wings thrown in for good measure.) Since both these animals were regarded as being extremely fierce and powerful, a combination of the two was even more frightening. They were said to be so big they could carry off a pair of horses in their claws.

If you wanted something even more out of the ordinary, you simply kept adding bits and pieces. The basilisk, for example, possessed the head and shoulders of a rooster, leathery wings like a bat and the tail of a snake. Although not all that big, it was certainly a nasty piece of work. Its breath was poisonous enough to split rocks apart, and it could kill with a single glance of its beady red eyes.

The chimaera was stranger still. It looked like a lion with a goat's head growing out the middle of its back and a snake where its tail should have been. It is such an unlikely looking beast that the name is now often used to describe something that can't possibly exist.

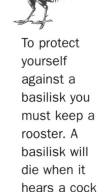

To protect yourself against a basilisk you must keep a rooster. A basilisk will die when it hears a cock crow.

The human angle

Sometimes, the scariest monsters are those that look something like ourselves.

A giant snake would be frightening enough, but we'd be a whole lot more frightened of one that was human from the waist up. That's what the ancient Greeks imagined Echidna, the mother of all monsters, to be like. She even made her daughters, the Gorgons, look good.

There is almost no limit to the number of legendary creatures that combine human and animal characteristics in this way. Centaurs had the head, chest and shoulders of a man and the body of a horse. Satyrs and fauns were part human and part goat.

The sphinx had a woman's head, the body of a dog, and the wings of a bird. One of her favourite hobbies was asking people riddles and eating anyone who couldn't answer them.

Perhaps the oddest creature of all was the manticore. This monster lived in the tropical areas of Asia. Not only did it combine the head of a man, the body of a lion and the tail of a scorpion, it could also shoot out poisonous spines and had three sets of razor-sharp teeth in its

According to Greek mythology, a centaur is a wild and beautiful creature, as strong as a stallion and as proud as a man.

mouth. No wonder an ancient Roman writer described it as "the most noxious animal that ever infested the earth"!

A hundred heads are better than one

A sure-fire recipe for creating monsters is to add extra arms and legs—or even heads, for that matter. The Greeks were

good at that. Among Echidna's many offspring was a three-headed dog named Cerberus, who guarded the gates of hell. Another of Echidna's sons, Geryon, had three heads and three bodies as well.

This, of course, was nothing compared to Echnida's husband, Typhon. With one hundred heads, he made everyone else in the family seem almost normal!

One hundred seems to have been a popular number among Greek monsters. There were hundred-handed giants, who fought a great battle against the gods, and a watchman with a hundred eyes named Argus. When he was killed, the queen of the gods took his eyes and put them in the tail of her favourite bird, the peacock.

Animal or vegetable?

Some imaginary creatures aren't so much frightening as downright weird.

Take the Lamb of Tartary for example. It looked much like an ordinary sheep, although its wool was a lot softer and whiter and could be woven into a cloth as smooth as silk. The big difference is that it is supposed to have grown on trees!

Well, not trees exactly. But they did grow from seeds. Once planted, these quickly sprouted into stalks about a metre (three feet) high, producing fruit exactly the same size and shape as a real lamb. The lambs remained attached to the stalk all their lives, feeding on nearby grass. When they had eaten everything within reach they just withered and died.

Understandably, the farmers were extremely fond of the "Vegetable Lambs". Not only were they good to eat, they didn't need shepherds to care for them!

In Scotland, there are similar legends about something called the "Tree Goose". This was said to produce large green fruit about the size of a melon. When the fruit was ripe, it fell into the sea and out hatched a little red and pink goose.

Strangely, any fruit that fell on the land didn't produce any geese at all. Although it was said to be extremely tasty!

Making it big in Hollywood

Monsters are just as popular today as they were thousands of years ago. They feature in endless numbers of novels, short stories, comic books and video games. Images of them are constantly stomping or slithering or oozing across our movie screens and television sets.

Although their names and faces may change, underneath they aren't really much different from those invented by the Greeks or during the Middle Ages.

A lot of them are simply scaled-up versions of everyday creatures. We've had giant ants, giant snakes, giant spiders, giant sharks, giant octopuses— even giant killer tomatoes! Perhaps the most famous film monster of them all, King Kong, is really just a big ape. (Although you wouldn't want to call him that to his face. Not when he's big enough to climb New York's Empire State Building as if it were a coconut tree and pluck fighter planes out of mid-air!)

Gorillas are the largest type of ape. They can grow to a height of 1.6 metres (5 ft 3 inches).

Godzilla may breathe fire and shoot lightning bolts from his eyes, but when you get right down to it, she's nothing more than an oversized lizard.

Personally, my favourite movie monster is Gamera, a tortoise the size of a skyscraper who featured in several Japanese science-fiction films made in the 1960s and 1970s. Whenever he needed to make a quick getaway, he would pull his legs inside his shell and blast off like a rocket. Whoever thought that one up certainly had a pretty wild imagination!

Out of this world

Monsters have to come from somewhere. For the ancient Greeks it was usually far-off countries like India and Africa. Nowadays, people visit these places all the time, so we need a new home for our monsters. Where better than outer space?

H.G. Wells was one of the first writers to come up with this idea. The Martians who invade Earth in his famous novel, *The War of the Worlds*, have a lot in common with Lovecraft's invisible, whistling octopus, including lots of

Lizards have scales on their skin for protection against predators and the environment. Mythical dragons were said to have scales and that was the reason why it was so hard to kill them.

tentacles and a nasty beaked mouth.

Edgar Rice Burroughs, on the other hand, invented a whole range of colourful creatures for stories like *The Princess of Mars*. Most have an extra pair of arms—except the hero's girlfriend. For some reason, she looks exactly like a beautiful earth-woman. I suppose four-armed Martians may be fun to fight, but you wouldn't want to marry one!

Like other monsters, most space creatures are either mixtures of animals or part man and part beast. Those in the *Alien* series of movies, for example, are a cross between insects and reptiles—and scary enough to give anyone nightmares. The *Star Wars* trilogy features everything from giant toads to elephant-headed drummers in a rock and roll band.

This little cockroach doesn't look very scary, but make it 50 times bigger and you might not want to see it in your room!

Do-it-yourself monsters

Believe it or not, you might actually have your own pet monster one day. The modern science of genetic engineering can already be used to create living things never before seen in nature.

It has mainly been done with plants, so far. Scientists have recently developed a blue rose by taking genes from another flower and combining them with those of an ordinary rose. You might wonder why they bother. After all, a blue rose isn't particularly useful. But it is different—and people around the world have paid good money to buy one of their own.

> **genetic engineering:** *changing the genes in the cells of plants and creatures to bring about a change in the offspring.*

The same techniques may one day be applied to animals as well. Chances are that some of these creatures would be the same sorts of fabulous beasts that have captured our imagination for so long. Imagine walking into a pet shop to buy a baby unicorn just as easily as you might buy a puppy or a goldfish!

In theory, you could even modify human beings this way. They could be given wings, for example, or claws like a lion—perhaps even lots of tentacles instead of two arms if we wanted to.

Let's just hope things don't ever go quite that far.

Here, there and everywhere

When you think about it, there are probably more monsters around nowadays than ever before—in books, movies and on television. Some are remarkably similar to creatures described in ancient myths and legends. Others combine bits and pieces from just about every animal, vegetable and mineral you can think of. Not one of them, however, looks like nothing anyone has ever seen before. If they did, we wouldn't be able to tell that they were monsters.

So, if something ever does crawl up out of your cellar one night, don't be surprised if it seems vaguely familiar.

Unless, of course, it happens to be an invisible, whistling octopus. In that case, you mightn't even know it's there until a tentacle reaches out and grabs you just as you're about to finish your last senten…

The cute, turtle-faced alien in Steven Spielberg's *E.T.* has helped make it the fourth highest money-earning film of all time.

chapter 3
Mistaken identity

Imagine...

W ILL BUNDLED his sealskin jacket more tightly around him. It was bitterly cold on deck, but he was tired of cleaning dishes and scouring pots. When cook had wanted someone to take warm ale to the lookouts, he'd jumped at the chance.

Now, he was beginning to think it mightn't have been such a good idea. The icy wind stung his face and his feet were already starting to go numb. He wondered how Tom and the others could have stayed up here so long without being frozen solid.

Tom was keeping watch at the bow, so Will visited him first.

"Thanks, lad," Tom said. He gulped down a few mouthfuls of steaming ale and smacked his lips loudly. "Ah! Warms the cockles of your heart, that does." He ruffled Will's hair. "So tell me," he said. "How are you enjoying life at sea? Still reckon you've done the right thing signing on?"

Will shrugged. "It's not exactly what I thought it would be," he admitted.

"Oh, yes?" Tom said. "Why's that?"

"Well, I figured it would be a bit more exciting." Will looked out across the sluggish water that just seemed to go on and on forever. "Not much to look at, is there?"

Tom laughed. "You never know," he said. "The oceans are full of wonders, lad. Keep your eyes peeled and there's no telling what you'll see."

Will couldn't imagine what. The only remarkable thing about the voyage so far was how many times he'd been sea-sick.

"Might even spot yourself a serpent," Tom told him. "I hear they're pretty common in these waters."

"Really?" Will looked at the sea more closely, trying to peer beneath the surface. "Ever seen one yourself, Tom?"

Tom shook his head. "But a fellow I shipped with a few years back knew someone who had. Great ugly beast it were. Two hundred paces long and as wide as a bell-tower. Would have pulled the whole ship down if they hadn't scared it off with a cannon."

Will shivered. "Hey, what's that?"

Tom turned to look. "What's what?" he asked.

"Over there," Will said. He pointed to a dark shape bobbing up and down in water nearby. "Looks like someone swimming."

"Nah," Tom told him. "It's too cold for that. You wouldn't last five minutes." He squinted, shading his eyes with one hand against the setting sun. Then he laughed. "Well, blow me down," he muttered. "It's a mermaid, lad! No mistake about it!"

"A mermaid?" Will peered more closely. The light was failing, so he couldn't see too clearly. But he supposed the shape did look a bit like that of a woman from the waist up.

"Hey, boys!" Tom shouted. "Come and look at this!"

One of the other lookouts rushed across to join them. The shape had drifted closer by now. Will could see its soft, brown eyes gazing up at them, and the wide, almost mischievous, smile on its face.

His heart thudded in his chest. It had to be a mermaid. Who else could have lived way out here, so far from land?

"Get a net!" Tom said. "We'll haul her aboard!"

Almost as he spoke, however, a sudden swell washed over her. Will glimpsed a sleek, forked tail skimming down through the water, then she was gone.

"Damn!" Tom said. "There's folks in London who'd have paid a fortune for her!" He slapped Will on the back. "Ah, well, lad, at least you'll have something to tell your grandchildren, eh?"

Will stared dreamily out across the empty sea. Yes, he thought. Yes, I will.

Perhaps a sailor's life wasn't going to be so boring after all.

THE END

THERE MAY NOT have been a cabin boy named Will on board the ship that encountered a mermaid off the coast of Russia in 1608, but a sailor named Thomas Hilles certainly was. The ship's captain, Henry Hudson, recorded details of the sighting in his logbook. He described the mermaid as human-sized, with long black hair hanging down her back. She had a tail like a porpoise that was "speckled like a mackerel".

Tales of mermaids are as old as mankind itself. Even in comparatively recent times, people have reported seeing them everywhere from Norway to the islands of the Pacific Ocean. Most of these stories are almost certainly made up. Other witnesses, however, like the two sailors on Hudson's ship, seem to have been telling the truth—or at least what they thought was the truth.

Obviously Thomas Hilles and his fellow crewmate, Robert Rayner, saw something in the water that evening. Henry Hudson was one of the most famous explorers of his time, and wouldn't have bothered mentioning the incident if he'd thought his men had simply been pulling his leg.

Is it possible they actually did see a mermaid? If not, why were they so convinced that they had?

From fantasy to fraud

Stories about creatures that were half human and half animal were common in ancient times. It was often their way of representing the forces of nature. A sea-god, for example, might have the tail of a fish. A sky-god might have wings like a bird. That's probably how legends about mermaids and mermen first started. But it doesn't explain why they have continued for so long.

If mermaids did exist, we'd certainly know about it. Either somebody would have photographed one or their bones would have been found washed up on the shore somewhere.

There have been plenty of phony mermaids put on display over the years. The most famous of these was the "Feejee Mermaid", which earned the American showman P.T. Barnum tens of thousands of dollars

One mermaid, supposedly caught by English fishermen in the 18th century, is said to have thought humans were very stupid because they threw away the water they boiled eggs in!

when he exhibited it in New York in 1842. It was less than a metre (three feet) long and didn't even vaguely resemble what most people imagined a mermaid to look like. Which isn't really surprising, as it was nothing more than the top half of a small monkey sewn onto the bottom half of a fish.

At the time, creating fake mermaids was big business among Japanese fishermen. One was sold in London for more than £20,000 ($40,000) during the 1830s. It's hard to imagine how anyone could have believed that these tiny, shrivelled corpses were the bodies of real mermaids, but thousands of people around the world paid to see them.

P.T. Barnum's "Feejee Mermaid". Would you believe this really existed?

Do mermaids really have whiskers?

Most likely, what so many sailors mistook for mermaids were actually sea-going mammals like the manatee and the dugong.

Both these creatures are only slightly larger than human beings, and their bodies taper from the waist down to a flat, flipper-like tail. The dugong, in particular, often suckles its young with the top half of its body sticking up out of the water while holding the baby to its breast with one flipper. Many reported sightings of "mermaids" describe them doing exactly the same thing. If disturbed, the animal will dive beneath the surface, often flicking its tail in the air in the process, just the way many "mermaids" are supposed to have done.

Of course, neither dugongs nor manatees are particularly pretty. When Christopher Columbus first saw some,

during his voyage to America in 1492, he noted in his log that "They are not as beautiful as they are painted." And no wonder. With their bulging eyes and squashed bristly noses, they certainly don't bear much resemblance to the glamorous beauties of myth and legend, let alone the star of Disney's *The Little Mermaid*.

Manatees are one of the world's endangered animals. There are probably no more than a thousand of them still living.

But, from a distance, a female dugong or manatee might well look human enough for some sailors to imagine they were actually gorgeous women with long, flowing hair. It wouldn't be the first time people had seen what they wanted to see, rather than what was actually there.

Serpent or squid?

Stories about sea-monsters are almost as common as those involving mermaids. Although details vary, these monsters generally take one of two forms. Some resemble gigantic serpents, like the one seen by crew members aboard the HMS *Daedalus* on 6 August 1848. In his official report of the incident, the ship's captain described the creature as being at least 20 metres (65 ft) long, with a large, snake-like head and "something like a mane of a horse" hanging down its back. Other monsters, including the legendary kraken, have tentacles like an octopus which are big enough to wrap around an entire ship and pull it under the sea.

In the days of sailing ships, sailors kept an uneasy eye out for the boiling of the ocean that indicated the presence of a kraken.

Strangely enough, both kinds may be based on the same real animal. Giant deep-sea squid have long tube-shaped bodies and a beaked mouth surrounded by ten snake-like tentacles. Very few of these creatures have ever been seen, because they spend most of their time at the bottom of the ocean. Specimens up to 17 metres (55 ft) long have been washed up on beaches, but they could possibly grow far larger than that, as none of the bodies found so far have been fully developed. The world's foremost expert on giant squid (which scientists call *Architeuthis*) estimates their maximum size could be about 45 metres (148 ft).

A giant squid drifting lazily on the surface with its tail out of the water could easily be mistaken for a tremendous serpent. Eight of their tentacles are quite thin and might look a bit like hair. This would explain why so many sea-serpents 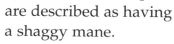 are described as having a shaggy mane.

We know giant squid sometimes attack boats because that is exactly what happened to some fishermen off the coast of Newfoundland in October 1873. Thinking the squid was a piece of

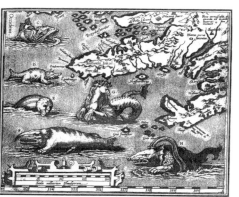

This 1570 map of Iceland shows some monsters that sailors thought they might meet.

wreckage, they tried to pull it towards them with a boathook. The squid rammed them with its beak and threw a tentacle around the boat. If twelve-year-old Tom Piccot hadn't hacked off the tentacle with an axe, they would have all been dragged under the water and killed.

This 6 metre (20 ft) long tentacle, by the

way, was the first solid evidence that giant squids actually existed. Up until then, all scientists had to go on were a few rotted remains and various bits and pieces found in the bellies of dead sperm whales. Giant squid apparently make up a large part of the sperm whales' diet. Just imagine what it would be like to see a battle to the death between a 15 tonne whale and a squid with tentacles 20 metres (65 ft) long!

Scientists estimate that the amount of giant squid eaten every year by sperm whales weighs more than the entire human race.

Fact versus fiction

One reason why people long ago found it easy to believe in non-existent animals is that hardly any of them ever travelled more than a few kilometres (a mile or so) from the village where they were born. As a result, they could only imagine what the rest of the world was like. To them, mermaids and unicorns were simply two more creatures they'd heard of but never seen—just like giraffes or elephants.

During the Middle Ages in Europe, for example, everything people knew about the world's animals was collected in books known as bestiaries. The writers of bestiary books made no attempt to find out whether the creatures they mentioned actually existed. Even the information they provided about quite real animals was often a mixture of fact and fable.

According to some bestiaries, lion cubs were born dead, and stayed that way until their fathers breathed life into them. Also, swans supposedly sang beautifully just before they died, even though hardly any of them can sing at all. Both swans and storks were also believed to take on human form when they migrated south for the winter.

Compared with tales like these, horned horses and women with fish's tails wouldn't have sounded strange at all!

Writers in the Middle Ages were called scribes. Books were written by hand and decorated with beautiful artwork.

How the unicorn got its horn

Many of the stories told about legendary animals during the Middle Ages were adapted from even older books written by the ancient Greeks and Romans. Often, these books only gave very sketchy details of the animals concerned, and so medieval authors used their imaginations to complete the picture.

The unicorn first described by a Greek writer named Ctesias in 400 B.C., for example, doesn't bear much resemblance to the magical creature listed in bestiaries. The "monoceros", as Ctesias called it, was extremely strong, and shaped more like a bull than a horse. It lived in India, and was so fierce that no one had ever managed to capture one. In fact, the only other animal that dared attack it at all was the elephant.

Now, as it happens, there was a strong, fierce, one-horned creature living in India at the time—the white rhinoceros. Of course, the rhinoceros' horn doesn't grow in the middle of its forehead, and it certainly isn't long and slender like a unicorn's. Over the years, however, people took the basic idea of a white, single-horned beast and turned it into something more glamorous.

The white rhinoceros cannot be domesticated. Humans like to hunt it because it is a dangerous animal.

Perhaps they were also influenced by the stories they heard about the Arabian oryx. The long, sharp horns of this cream-coloured antelope are so straight that if travellers saw the creature side-on, they could easily have thought that it only had one horn instead of two.

Medieval writers combined elements of these two very real animals and came up with a mythical, horse-like beast with a single spiral horn and magical powers. Strangely enough, though we know that unicorns are not real, that's still how we picture them to this very day.

According to legend, the horn of a unicorn could render poison harmless. Ancient kings, in constant danger of being poisoned by their subjects, would pay well for one of these horns.

Heads or hands?

At first glance, it's hard to think of any living creature resembling the Hydra. This legendary Greek monster had nine heads, the middle one of which was supposed to be immortal. Every time one of its heads was cut off, two more grew in its place. The famous hero Hercules finally destroyed the beast by burning away eight of the heads and burying the immortal one under a large rock.

If you went to the Vatican museum in Rome, however, and looked at the marble tablet they have there showing Hercules fighting the Hydra, you'd notice it looks very much like a large octopus. Eight of the heads, of course, are the tentacles surrounding its real or "immortal" one.

Octopuses are common in the waters around Greece and can have tentacles up to a metre and half (five feet) long. Such a creature could be extremely dangerous, and the hydra was no doubt based on stories of them occasionally attacking fishermen.

The octopus is also able to grow replacement tentacles if any are bitten off. This would explain the Hydra's legendary ability to sprout new heads.

The monster in the maze

The older stories are, the more muddled they can become. Greek mythology tells of a creature with the body of a man and the head of a bull that used to live in the middle of a huge maze on the island of Crete. The minotaur, as it was called, lived on human flesh. Seven young men and seven beautiful maidens sent as a tribute from the Greek city of Athens were fed to it each year. A hero named Theseus eventually hunted the minotaur down in its maze (which the Greeks called a labyrinth) and killed it.

A number of half-remembered facts about ancient Crete probably contributed to this legend. We now know that the Cretans sometimes sacrificed children to their gods. We also know that one of the most important of these gods was worshipped in the form of a bull.

That explains the bull-headed monster eating young Athenians. But what about the maze? In Greek, the word "labyrinth" actually means something like House of the Double-Axe. Archaeological excavations in Crete have unearthed huge palaces many thousands of years old. The largest of these, at a place called Knossos, had several hundred rooms, some of them with carvings of double-bladed axes on the walls. So, it's likely that the labyrinth in which the minotaur lived was actually the palace of Knossos, which must have seemed like a huge, baffling maze to any ancient Greeks who saw it.

> According to legend, the span of the minotaur's horns was wider than a man's outstretched arms.

Still making the same mistakes?

People's eyes often play tricks on them. Also, it's easy to be misled by what someone else thinks they saw, or if a story has been passed down through several generations. No doubt, that's how many tales about non-existent creatures started—and how they still start today.

> Surveys show that well over 50% of American people believe that aliens from outer space regularly visit the earth.

Every year, thousands of UFO sightings are reported around the world. In most, if not all, cases there is nothing all that mysterious about these objects. They might be comets, aeroplane lights, even balls of lightning. But many people remain convinced that they are flying saucers belonging to aliens from outer space.

Like mermaids and other legendary creatures, these aliens have taken on a life of their own. Eye-witness reports of encounters with them are published in books and newspapers. Countless films are made about them. And yet there is no proof whatsoever that they actually exist.

In the end, of course, it doesn't make much difference. Aliens will always be real to people who believe in them—just the way mermaids were.

chapter 4
Living proof

Imagine...

Rapid City Gazette
Monday, 18 May 2000

Big Foot snapped by local scouts!

TWO MEMBERS of the 3rd Rapid River Scout Troop claim to have stumbled across the legendary ape-man known as Big Foot while camping at Rapid River National Park. The pair, Jack Carter, aged 14, and Dwayne Richardson, 15, even have a photograph to prove it.

The encounter took place late Saturday afternoon after they discovered several large footprints beside a stream in the nearby woods. "They were twice the size of ours," Dwayne said. "At least thirty centimetres (a foot) long and almost as wide. We thought they were bear tracks."

Dwayne and Jack found more footprints leading into the woods, and decided to see where they went. After following the tracks for about a kilometre (half a mile), they finally caught up with their owner in a small clearing.

"It was just standing there," Jack said. "Eating berries off one of the trees. Dwayne managed to take a photo before it saw us and took off."

According to the boys, the creature resembled a giant ape covered in long, reddish-yellow hair, and was well over two and a half metres (eight feet) tall.

The International Society of Cryptozoology (a world-wide organisation devoted to investigating reports of new or unknown animals) intends to conduct a thorough search of the area as soon as possible. A spokesman for the group claimed similar creatures have been sighted numerous times in the forests of north California over the past forty years. "They can't all be false alarms," he said. "Big Foot is obviously out there somewhere—and sooner or later we're going to find him."

BIG FOO'

PID RIVER. Two boys
ndered away to inv
~~ towards the
anaged

Local park rangers don't agree. "I've been working here twenty years," Frank Kirby said. "If there were any ape-men about, I reckon I'd know about it. Them boys probably just never seen a bear standing up on his hind legs before and got a bit confused."

Experts from the Wildlife Department who have examined both the footprints and Jack's photo are equally sceptical. "The tracks are entirely consistent with those of an adult brown bear," Dr Samuel Alderton said. "As for the photograph—well, the quality is so poor it could be just about anything. But large bears certainly aren't unknown in the Rapid River area at this time of year."

Jack and Dwayne remain convinced that the creature was none other than Big Foot himself.

"I know a bear when I see one," Dwayne said. "This was something else."

The boys plan to continue camping out at the park in future, but say they have no intention of trying to hunt down the creature themselves. "I feel kind of sorry for the poor guy," Jack said. "He seemed more scared of us than we were of him. I guess all he really wants is to be left alone."

THE END

I MAY HAVE invented the *Rapid City Gazette*, but similar stories appear quite regularly in newspapers all over the world. And it isn't just hairy ape-men that people claim to see. Others report sighting giant, long-necked lake monsters. Or flying reptiles. Or even stranger creatures such as the so-called Jersey Devil, which was described as having "a head like a collie and a face like a horse".

Unfortunately, like Dwayne and Jack, none of these eyewitnesses ever seem able to back up their stories with hard evidence. We just have to take their word for it. Which is why most scientists believe the creatures they describe are just as imaginary as mermaids.

Cryptozoologists aren't so sure. "Crytpo" is an ancient Greek word meaning secret or hidden. Zoologists are people who study animals. So cryptozoologists study secret or hidden animals—in other words, ones that have not been proven to exist. They take these reported sightings seriously and try to work out what the people involved may actually have seen.

cryptozoologist: *someone who searches for previously undiscovered animals.*

53

But if creatures like the one in Dwayne and Jack's story really do exist, what on earth are they?

Survival stories

Cryptozoologists believe that there are some animals, assumed by everyone else to have died out millions of years ago, which might still survive in various parts of the world. If this was true, monsters like the one supposedly living in Scotland's Loch Ness could be some kind of dinosaur.

Hairy giants like the North American Big Foot, and similar creatures reportedly sighted elsewhere in the world, could belong to ancient species of apes.

Of course, that's all a pretty big maybe. But, perhaps the idea isn't quite as crazy as it sounds.

Crocodiles, sharks and turtles all existed long before the age of the dinosaurs, and have survived into the present day more or less unchanged. There are also quite recent examples of creatures thought to be extinct suddenly turning up alive and well.

In 1938, when South African

extinct: *no longer existing on earth.*

fishermen reported catching a two metre (6 ft 6 inch) fish unlike any they'd ever seen before, scientists were amazed to discover it was actually a coelacanth (pronounced *see-la-kanth*). Until then, everyone had believed this must have died out with the dinosaurs. And yet, there it was, as large as life, looking exactly the way it did in fossils dating back 70 million years.

The coelacanth is found in the waters off southern Africa.

If the coelacanth is still around, then other ancient creatures might be as well. The only question is, how have they managed to go unnoticed for so long?

fossils:

traces of ancient life such as bones, shells and footprints found in rocks.

Ends of the Earth

One answer could be that they inhabit very remote and hard-to-get-at places like mountains and jungles.

The world is not as well explored as most people think. A lot of what we see on maps is based on aerial photographs, or even pictures taken by satellites up in space. They show major features like rivers and mountains, but don't really tell us anything about the sort of creatures that might live there.

Large parts of Africa are covered in rainforest so dense that you could fly right over it without even glimpsing what was hidden beneath. Even something as large as an elephant could go completely unnoticed. The same is true of the Amazon Basin in South America, which one 20th century explorer described as "a vast night of trees" covering 5.5 million sq km (2.12 million sq miles).

Other areas in South America are even more inaccessible. In Venezuela, flat-topped mountains known as mesas are cut off from the rest of the world by sheer cliffs between 1000 and 3000 metres (3280 to 9840 ft) above the jungle floor. Some mesas are more than thirty kilometres (eighteen miles) long and have never been properly explored. It wasn't until 1937 that anyone discovered that one of them contained the highest waterfall in the world.

If a 980 metre (3214 ft) waterfall can go unnoticed for

rainforest:

thick evergreen forest found in regions of high humidity and rainfall.

so long, there's no telling what unknown creatures might be hidden there.

The world is full of surprises

There are certainly plenty of animals out there left to be discovered.

Thousands of new ones are identified every year. Most of these are pretty small, of course, like insects, slugs and worms. But much larger creatures also crop up from time to time.

In November 1976, for example, the US Navy research ship AFB-14 discovered a previously unknown type of shark near one of the Hawaiian islands. It was over three metres (ten feet) long and weighed 745 kg (1639 lb). Because of its huge mouth and floppy, rubbery lips, scientists nicknamed the creature "Megamouth". The reason no one had ever seen one before is because they apparently live in very deep water and have no reason to ever come to the surface.

A new kind of whale was found as recently as 1991. Another has been sighted at least 24 times in the eastern Pacific

Scientists used to think there were about one-and-a-half million different kinds of animals in the world. Latest estimates, however, put the figure at around 20 times that many.

Ocean, although no one has caught one yet.

Several large land animals have also been discovered in recent times. The jungles of Vietnam have produced at least five over the past few years. These include a barking deer and the spindlehorn, which one scientist described as a "kind of goat, but a little bit strange".

Legends come to life

Every zoo contains a whole list of animals that were either completely unknown or regarded as mere legends until quite recent times.

When Europeans first heard rumours about "terrible hairy men" who were supposed to live in the African jungle, they thought the natives were simply making things up. It wasn't until 1847 that two American missionaries finally proved that the creatures actually existed. They were, of course, gorillas which are the largest apes on the planet.

The world's largest lizard wasn't discovered until 1912.

missionary:

someone who travels to a remote place to teach religion.

A pilot whose plane crash-landed on the small island of Komodo, part of what is now Indonesia, reported having seen ferocious 4 metre (13 ft) dragons while he was there. Naturally, nobody believed a word he said. Not long after, however, an expedition to the island returned with live specimens to back up his story. They aren't actually dragons, of course, just very big lizards. But they are still powerful enough to kill full-grown buffaloes and wild pigs.

The komodo isn't the only lizard that's called a dragon. This water dragon lizard lives in Australia.

It wasn't until 1937 that Westerners first glimpsed the giant panda. Until then, the cuddly black and white bear was thought to only exist in Chinese legends.

Discoveries like these give hope to those who still dream of tracking down other unknown animals one day.

Scotland's shyest star

Just about everybody has heard of the Loch Ness monster.

This mysterious creature has been spotted on and off for more than thirteen hundred years. The first reported sighting dates back to the 6th century.

Nessie, as it is called, has become a huge tourist attraction in recent times. There is an Official Loch Ness Monster Exhibition Centre where you can see multimedia displays about the creature.

The gift shop sells tee-shirts, postcards and just about everything else you can think of with Nessie pictures plastered all over them. Outside, there is an artificial pond where a large coin-operated model of the monster swims around whenever someone puts money in the slot.

Loch Ness is not the only lake in Scotland to harbour a monster. A similar monster has been sighted in Loch Morar as well.

It isn't just tourists who look for Nessie in this northern Scottish lake, which is 36 km (22 miles) long. Scientists have used underwater radar and midget submarines to probe its secrets. But we still have no idea whether a monster actually lives there or not, let alone what it might be.

Last of the dinosaurs?

Nessie may be the most famous lake monster in the world, but she certainly isn't the only one. A similar creature has reportedly been seen many times in the waters of Cadboro Bay in Canada. It has been given the scientific name cadborosaurus, although most people just call it "Caddy".

In fact, North America is well supplied with monsters. They have been spotted in more than 90 different lakes and rivers. Lake Okanagan in British Columbia has one named "Ogopogo", while Lake Champlain's is known as "Champ". Others have reportedly been spotted in many other countries, including Ireland, Sweden, Russia, and Turkey.

All these creatures are usually described as having long, snake-like necks, humped backs, and paddle-shaped flippers. They seem to vary in length from 10 to 20 metres (33 to 66 ft).

Cryptozoologists point out that sea-going creatures, very similar to this description, lived millions of years ago during the age of the dinosaurs. They are called plesiosaurs. These were air-breathing reptiles, so they had to stick their heads out of the water every so often to breath. Nessie and her North American cousins are usually spotted doing exactly the same thing.

An unsolved mystery

Could plesiosaurs have survived in a few isolated lakes the way coelacanths have in the world's oceans?

Most scientists don't think so. They point out that there simply isn't enough food in a place like Loch Ness to feed anything weighing more than about three hundred kilograms (six hundred and sixty pounds). In their opinion, it's much more likely that what the Nessie people claim to have seen is nothing more than a large fish or eel—or even a half-submerged log!

Nessie's supporters suggest that there may be underground waterways linking the loch to the sea. That would mean the monster could come and go as she liked. Some even think she might travel overland. She has reportedly been sighted on dry land several times. In 1933, a couple claimed they had to stop their car for her while she crossed the road in front of them!

The mystery of Loch Ness will probably never be solved. The only way to prove for certain that Nessie doesn't exist would be to completely drain the lake. Even then, it could be said that she just didn't happen to be there at the time.

One thing is certain, thousands of people will continue to visit Loch Ness every year in the hope of seeing this famous monster with their own eyes.

An African dinosaur?

Mokele-Mbembe (pronounced *mo-kay-lee mmm-bem-bee*) is quite a mouthful. In recent times, reports of this mysterious dinosaur-like creature have attracted a great deal of interest. Several people have already gone looking for the beast in the dense African jungle where it supposedly lives, with more expeditions planned for the near future.

The rainforests of Central Africa certainly seem a far more likely place to find dinosaurs than ice-cold rivers and lakes. Its hot, wet climate hasn't changed much for sixty million years or so, and many of the plants that grow there are virtually identical to the ones ancient dinosaurs fed on. After all,

Mokele-Mbembe on the attack!

crocodiles appeared in the region around the same time, and they're still going strong. Couldn't it then be possible that at least one or two species of dinosaur have survived as well?

According to the Pygmies who inhabit these forests, Mokele-Mbembe lives in remote swamps and rivers. They say it is about the size of an elephant with a snake-like neck and a long, powerful tail.

Some drawings of Mokele-Mbembe show a long horn in the middle of its head, but this is said to belong to another animal known as Emela-ntouka or killer of elephants. There is no real proof that these creatures exist at all.

The only past or present animals that fit this description are sauropod dinosaurs like the diplodocus. That's why people were so excited when they heard about it.

Unfortunately, so far no one has been able to prove that the creature actually exists. Investigators have found a few unidentified footprints in the area, but no bones or other remains. Perhaps we'll never know for sure one way or the other. Like the Loch Ness monster, however, the hunt for Mokele-Mbembe is bound to fascinate people around the world for many years to come.

Riddles in the snow

Eric Shipton never did succeed in being the first man to climb the world's highest mountain. But when he returned from Mt Everest in 1951, he did become famous for a very different reason.

The photographs of huge footprints that he brought back from the Himalayan mountains were regarded as the first real proof that the legendary Yeti or Abominable Snowman actually existed.

The footprints Shipton found were the same basic shape as a man's, but over thirty centimetres (twelve feet) long. He followed the trail for more than sixteen hundred metres (one mile) before it finally disappeared down a steep slope.

Other mountain climbers in the region have reported seeing similar tracks. Not only are the footprints longer and wider than human ones, they are also sunk much more deeply into the snow.

This suggests they were made by something several times heavier than a man. If they are those of a yeti, the creature must stand at least two and a half metres (eight feet) tall and weigh around half a tonne.

According to the people of Tibet, Abominable Snowmen are giant man-like creatures who live in caves high up in the mountains. Their bodies are covered in thick coats of dark brown hair. They have oval-shaped heads running to a point at the top, and white, hairless faces a bit like that of a gorilla.

This description is amazingly similar to that of many other ape-men reported to exist elsewhere in the world.

Big Foot & Co.

Big Foot is so famous in north-west USA that one county has passed a law making it illegal for anyone to kill one. This is despite the fact that there is no proof that anyone has ever actually seen one.

Australia has its Yowies. To the native Indian of British Columbia in Canada they are Sasquatch. In China they are called Yeren. The Nguoi Rung or Wildman is said to inhabit the mountains of Vietnam.

Cryptozoologists believe these may all be related to a species of

Australian researcher Rex Gilroy has collected more than 3000 reported sightings of Yowies in Australia. It is usually described as looking a bit like a gorilla, with a black shiny face and big yellow eyes.

primitive man-like ape called *Gigantopithecus*. Judging by the size of their teeth and other remains, these giant creatures must have been around three metres (ten feet) tall and would have weighed twice as much as an adult male gorilla. In other words, its footprints would probably have been exactly the same size as those of Big Foot or the Abominable Snowman.

The only problem is that *Gigantopithecus* seems to have died out 500,000 years ago. Most likely it was killed off by mankind's early ancestors, who were smaller but much more intelligent.

But who knows? Perhaps some do still survive in remote parts of the world. If so, we are bound to track them down sooner or later. Something almost as tall as a basketball ring and as heavy as a small car can't hide forever!

The photo that fooled the world

One of the biggest problems cryptozoologists face is that not everyone tells the truth. In fact, on investigation, some famous reports of unknown

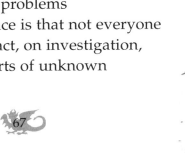

animals have turned out to be fakes.

In 1934, for example, an English doctor named R. Kenneth Wilson produced a photograph he claimed to have taken while visiting Loch Ness. It clearly showed a long-necked animal swimming in the water. The Surgeon's Photograph, as it was called, made Nessie an international star. It seemed to prove once and for all that there was some kind of strange creature living in the lake, even if no one could be sure what it was.

We now know, however, that the whole thing was an elaborate hoax dreamed up by a man with the unlikely name of Marmaduke Arundel Wetherell.

Wetherell had been sent to Loch Ness by an English newspaper to investigate reports of a monster being seen there. When he couldn't find anything, he decided to make his own by sticking a head and neck, which were 30cm (1 ft) long and made of plastic and wood, onto a toy submarine. Wetherell then took a picture of the model and had Dr Wilson send it to the newspaper. Wetherell reasoned that if the picture came from a doctor it was more likely

hoax:

a trick or practical joke designed to fool people into believing something that isn't true.

to be accepted as genuine.

The truth behind the Surgeon's Photograph remained a secret for 60 years. It was finally revealed by Wetherell's stepson, Christian Spurling, shortly before he died in November 1993.

The glyptodont is an extinct mammal. Its body was such a mixture of bits and pieces, it's hard to believe this is not a monster created for a movie.

So, the thousands of books and articles that were written trying to explain exactly what the photograph shows are based on nothing more than a few scraps of tin and plastic probably still lying somewhere in the waters of Loch Ness where Wetherell left them more than 65 years ago!

Fact or fiction?

A lot of the reports of unknown animals investigated by cryptozoologists are probably just cases of mistaken identity. Others may be outright lies. But that still leaves a few that might actually have some truth to them. If they're not investigated, how would we ever know?

Perhaps one day, like Dwayne and Jack, you will come face to face with one of these legendary creatures yourself. Then, at least you would know for sure that they really do exist!

In the meantime, the only way to separate fact from fiction is by examining the evidence and trying to keep as open a mind as possible.

A Canadian prospector named Albert Ostman claimed he was kidnapped by a Big Foot family in 1924 and held prisoner for several days.

As one cryptozoologist says, "We're not just wasting our time looking for new animals. There are still a number of mysteries out there—that's what makes it so fascinating."

chapter 5
Lost worlds

Imagine...

Maui HAD never been this deep into the forest before. The trees grew thicker and taller with every step, their emerald leaves almost blotting out the sun.

It was the first time he had been allowed to join the hunt. Until now, he'd always had to wait at home with the women while the warriors went in search of the Great Red Bird. He held his spear tightly, trying to remember everything his father had told him.

Te Kuru was big and strong. It could kill with a single blow. Maui had seen hunters with legs shattered and bellies ripped open by its terrible claws.

Suddenly, Maui's father held up his hand. Something was moving behind a thick clump of bushes up ahead. He motioned for the hunters to spread out. They obeyed silently, forming a long line to either side.

"There!" his father shouted.

The hunters broke into a run, shouting and banging their spears together.

Maui scrambled to keep up. He glimpsed a brightly coloured crest in the underbrush, then it disappeared. For a moment, he thought the giant bird had escaped, then he saw it again, lumbering clumsily through the trees.

The hunters followed, but at a safe distance. They needed to wait until they reached open ground before closing in for the kill. Then they would be able to surround the creature and attack it from all sides at once. Even the strongest warrior couldn't hope to bring down something as big as Te Kuru on his own.

They were in luck. The forest slowly began to thin out. Soon they were jogging through knee-high grass rather than picking their way through tightly-packed trees. A river lay just ahead, cutting off the bird's retreat.

With nowhere to run, Te Kuru turned to face them. Stretched to its full height, it

was at least twice as tall as Maui's father
and looked much heavier than anything
the hunters had brought back in the past.
Its long neck waved menacingly from
side to side as it glared down at them
with huge orange eyes.

Now came the dangerous part. Some of
the hunters darted forward, jabbing at the
bird with their spears. Quick as a flash, Te
Kuru lashed out with one giant foot. A
hunter fell, howling with pain. Maui
could see blood pouring from his face.

Everyone was shouting and screaming.
A few spears had found their mark, but
Te Kuru was still on its feet, towering
above the ring of hunters like a feathered
giant surrounded by children.

Then Maui saw his chance. Te Kuru was supporting all its weight on one leg, having just aimed another kick at a nearby hunter. Almost without thinking, Maui darted in and smashed his spear into its knee. There was a loud crack. Next thing he knew, Te Kuru toppled to the ground as its leg buckled beneath it.

The other hunters quickly closed in for the kill. Te Kuru thrashed and squawked as the spears struck home, then fell silent.

The Great Red Bird was dead.

Maui joined the other hunters to cut up the mighty beast. Not a scrap of it would be wasted. Its feathers would decorate his father's war-cloak. Its bones would be turned into fish-hooks. Its skull would make a fine holder for tattooing powder.

Best of all, their tribe would feast well that night—and for many nights to come.

Maui felt someone grab his shoulder. He looked up to see his father standing over him.

"I did it, father!" he said. "I brought down the Te Kuru with my spear!"

His father smiled. "I know. May it be the first of many."

Maui's heart swelled with pride. "Oh, it will be, Father," he said. "It will be."

THE END

M AUI WOULD have been disappointed. By the time the Maori people arrived in New Zealand 700 years ago the Great Red Bird, or moa as we call it, had almost completely died out. The few that remained were soon killed off, not only by Maori hunters, but also by the dogs and rats that came with them.

As well as being the tallest birds that ever lived, moas were also one of the strangest. They couldn't fly because they were much too big and heavy. Unlike other flightless birds, however, such as ostriches and emus, they had no traces of wings or tails whatsoever. Nor did they have fully-developed feathers, just thin, silky ones that looked almost like hair.

Its distant cousin, the kiwi, still lives in New Zealand today. Although only about the size of a chicken, kiwis also lack wings and tails, and have the same hair-like feathers as moas. As far as we know, no other bird in the world has ever looked anything like them.

An island paradise

Imagine a place where all animals lived peacefully together. Where there were no snakes. No crocodiles. No lions or tigers. No birds of prey like hawks or eagles.

Sounds like paradise, doesn't it?

That's exactly what New Zealand was like when the first human settlers landed there around A.D. 1200.

Because the islands of New Zealand had been cut off from the rest of the world for hundreds of millions of years, the mammals that became common

everywhere else on earth never reached there. Birds had the place almost to themselves. With no enemies to fly away from, they gradually lost the use of their wings. Flying took a lot of energy. It was a lot easier for them to just walk wherever they wanted to go.

Kiwis can only be found in New Zealand. They are a protected species.

Some, like the moa, grew to be quite enormous. Others developed very strange habits. One kind of parrot, known as the kakapo, not only stopped flying, but also took up living in burrows like a rabbit.

Unfortunately, many of New Zealand's weird and wonderful native animals have now disappeared. When Europeans began settling the country from the late

1700s onwards, they brought 168 different kinds of birds and mammals with them. These included everything from deer, rabbits and sheep to blackbirds and sparrows. Having been isolated for so long, native species were unable to compete with these more resilient newcomers.

The native birds and animals either dwindled significantly in numbers or were wiped out altogether.

Even New Zealand's national symbol, the kiwi, is rarely sighted in the wild today. No more than a few hundred kakapos still survive.

And the moa, of course, is gone forever.

> The tuatara lizard of New Zealand is the only living creature to still have traces of a third eye in the middle of its forehead—something which disappeared in other animals hundreds of millions of years ago!

The truth behind a legend?

What sort of bird lays an egg 30 cm (1 ft) long and 20 cm (8 inches) wide? That's what the director of the Paris zoo wanted to know when three of them were sent to him from the African island of Madagascar in 1850. He imagined something like an ostrich, only as tall as a two storey-house. He named the creature

Aepyornis maximus, which means the tallest of the high birds, even though no one had ever seen one.

There were, however, legends about a giant bird living on Madagascar. It was called the ruhk (pronounced *roc*). Sinbad the Sailor is supposed to have seen one when he was shipwrecked on the island. The ruhks were said to be so big they could lift full-grown elephants in their claws and carry them into the air.

Aepyornis maximus wasn't quite that large. It couldn't fly either, so there isn't much chance of one ever having carried off an elephant—or anything else for that matter. But it was certainly big enough to do it, weighing around six hundred kilograms (one thousand, three hundred and twenty pounds).

According to Marco Polo, the ruhk's outstretched wings were big enough to blot out the sun.

Gone—but not quite forgotten

Unlike its relatives elsewhere in the world, Madagascar's elephant bird must have survived until quite recent times.

Certainly long enough to inspire legends about the ruhk. A few may even still have been alive in the mid-nineteenth century, when the first of their eggs were discovered. Native families at the time used them as water containers, but said they were "very, very rarely" found any more. By that stage, there were probably only a handful of the birds still living on the entire island.

So, why did the elephant bird disappear? For once, it seems humans weren't to blame. The local people never hunted it for food. In fact, apart from taking the occasional egg, they left it pretty much in peace. Most likely, it died out because of changes in the climate that dried up the swamps where it lived.

Whatever the reason, it was gone before any European ever saw one. All that remains are a few skeletons, some enormous eggs, and the legend of a giant bird whose wings blotted out the sun.

> Elephant bird eggs were so big that just one of them would make an omelette large enough to feed 75 people!

The world's weirdest wildlife?

Australia is home to some of the strangest animals in the world. It hasn't been isolated as long as New Zealand, so early forms of mammals managed to reach there. But these weren't replaced by more advanced species as happened in most other places.

When the Europeans arrived in Australia, they couldn't believe their eyes. The animals they found were unlike anything they'd ever seen before. They had trouble even describing them. Early explorers, for example, reported seeing a large animal with the head of a deer and a long tail. It not only stood on its hind-legs like a bird, but could also hop like a frog. Imagine what people back in Europe must have pictured the animal to look like. No wonder they thought it couldn't possibly exist.

What the explorers saw, of course, were kangaroos. They were just one of many bizarre creatures inhabiting the new land.

Perhaps strangest of all was a weird little animal discovered in Queensland in 1797. When its skin was sent to England, scientists thought it must have been a fake, like the Japanese mermaids which were popular around the same time. Surely someone had attached a duck's bill to the body of a small, furry mammal.

They examined the body carefully, but couldn't find any trace of glue or stitches. Apparently it was a real animal after all. They named it *Ornithorhynchus paradoxus*—the paradoxical animal with a bird's beak. Most of us just call it the platypus.

Giants of an ancient race

If European settlers thought kangaroos and platypuses were strange, it's a good thing they didn't arrive thousands of years earlier. Back then, Australia's wildlife was even weirder.

It was a lot bigger too. *Dromornis*, for example, was the largest bird ever to walk the earth. It stood 3.5 metres (11 ft 6 inches) tall and weighed over half a tonne. You would have needed a sledge-hammer to break open one of its eggs. The shells were more than four centimetres (one and a half inches) thick!

There were plenty of giant mammals as well. Some kangaroos were almost twice the size they are nowadays and weighed around three hundred kilograms (six

It took scientists almost a hundred years to work out whether the Australian platypus was a reptile or a mammal.

hundred and sixty pounds). Biggest of all was the *Diprotodon*. This looked a bit like a wombat, but was as big as a rhinoceros.

Australia was much greener and wetter in those days. There was plenty of food

for these giant animals to eat. As the climate changed, however, life became more difficult for them. The arrival of the first Australian Aborigines, probably about 40,000 years ago, may have sealed their fate. Giant, slow-moving creatures like the *Diprotodon* would have been easy prey for the hunters.

Fortunately, Australia is a big country. While the *Diprotodon* and other giants may have gone, not all traces of the ancient marsupial world has been lost. It lives on in the kangaroos, wombats, koalas and countless other creatures that still delight us today.

Aboriginal elders were responsible for teaching hunting skills to the young men of the tribe.

Frozen in time

Not all the giants of the past have disappeared completely. At least one can still be seen from time to time, even though it has been extinct for thousands of years.

Imagine a shaggy-haired elephant with huge curved tusks up to five metres (sixteen and a half feet) long. That's what mammoths looked like. Great herds of them once roamed the frozen plains of northern Europe during the last Ice Age. They were so well suited to the cold that they couldn't adapt when the climate began to warm up again, and gradually died out altogether. The arrival of human hunters twelve thousand years ago probably didn't help either.

The mammoth was named after the mammantu, a legendary beast of northern Europe.

Some mammoths, however, were snap frozen in the ice. Several dozen of these have been discovered over the past few hundred years. Their bodies are perfectly preserved, just like food from the freezer compartment of your refrigerator. When Dr Otto F. Hertz discovered one in North-East Russia in 1900, its meat was still fresh enough to feed his sledge dogs. He even ate a piece himself!

A legend reborn?

When natives found the carcasses of mammoths half-buried in the ice, they thought the animals had only just died.

Legends spread about giant rats or moles, living in burrows under the snow, that were struck dead the moment they reached the surface. These legendary beasts were known as mammantu, which is how the mammoth originally got its name.

There may not be any mammoths living under the ground. But perhaps one day they will make a comeback on it.

mammantu:

that which lives beneath the ground.

clone:

an exact copy of a plant or animal grown from a single cell.

In September 1999, a French explorer named Bernard Buigues succeeded in cutting a whole mammoth from the ice in the far north of Russia. Rather than letting it de-frost, he transported it by helicopter to some nearby caves. That way, scientists will be able to examine it closely before the body starts to decay.

There is even a chance that genetic engineering can be used to produce a perfect copy, or clone, of this vanished giant. Sheep have already been cloned this way, but no one knows whether it can be done with something that has been frozen for so long.

If they are successful, maybe mammoths will soon walk the earth once

more, just as they did a hundred
centuries ago!

Dead as a dodo

Dodos haven't been gone as long as
many other lost creatures. But they are
certainly gone forever.

Just four hundred years ago, they were
very much alive. They lived
on the remote island of
Mauritius, 900 km (540 miles) east
of Africa. Although only about the
size of a large turkey, they were far
too heavy to fly. In fact, they were so
fat they couldn't manage more than a
slow waddle. They are often
described as being stupid as well, because
they didn't even try to run away from
hunters. Actually, they were just very
trusting. If you grew up on a remote
island with no natural predators, you'd
probably behave the same way.

Unfortunately, when predators
did arrive on Mauritius in 1598, the
dodos were completely defenceless.
Portuguese and Dutch sailors
slaughtered thousands of the birds
for their meat. Dogs and rats

predator:
*animal that lives
by hunting and
eating other
creatures.*

brought by the new settlers feasted on dodo eggs and the young chicks. Within a few years, they had become so scarce that visitors to the island had trouble finding them.

Dutch settlers called dodos "walghvogels" which means "disgusting birds". Our name for them comes from the Portuguese word "doudo", which means "simpleton".

The last living dodo was seen in 1681. The next time anybody bothered to look for one, twelve years later, there were none to be found. By 1750, the island's inhabitants had forgotten that the bird ever existed.

People in the rest of the world were shocked when they realised what had happened. None of the dodos brought back to Europe had survived. There wasn't even a stuffed specimen in any of the world's museums.

Less than a hundred years after being discovered, the dodo had completely vanished from the face of the earth.

How many others will follow?

Scientists estimate that more than a hundred different kinds of animals become extinct every day. The majority disappear almost without anyone noticing. Most are insects and tiny sea animals that only a few experts knew about to begin with. But the fact remains that species are dying out faster nowadays than they have at any other period of time in the past 65 million years.

They aren't being hunted to extinction like the dodo. They aren't the victims of a changing climate like mammoths and *Diprotodons*. There simply isn't enough room in the world for them any more.

Six billion people take up a lot of space. Huge areas of land are constantly being cleared to make way for towns and cities. Even more land is being turned into farms to feed the world's ever-increasing population. That means there is less and less wilderness for animals to live in.

Organisations like the World Wide Fund for Nature are doing what they can to save endangered animals. But it may already be too late for many of them. Although more than 3500 parks and other protected areas have been set up around the world, these still only make up 3 per cent of the earth's total land area. Everywhere else, thousands of creatures

The giant panda is on the world's endangered species list.

are being driven to extinction at a frightening rate.

To our grandchildren, giant pandas, tigers, rhinoceroses and many other animals found in zoos today may have disappeared forever.

And the world will be a much poorer place without them. The fact is, no matter how fantastic imaginary creatures may be, they aren't nearly as wonderful as the real thing.

The black rhinoceros is one of the world's most endangered animals. It is killed for its horn, which fetches between $16,000 and $22,000 US per kilogram in Asian markets.

Where to from here?

If you're interested in learning more about giants, unicorns and other imaginary creatures, there are literally thousands of books available on the subject. Here are a few that are well worth looking at: *The Book of Fabulous Beasts* by Joseph Nigg, *Zoo of the Gods* by Anthony S. Mercatante and *Out of This World* by Michael Page and Robert Ingpen.

Budding cryptozoologists should check out *Living Wonders* by John Mitchell and Robert J.M. Rickard, and *Creatures From Elsewhere* by Peter Brookesmith. These will tell you all you could possibly want to know about Big Foot, the Loch Ness monster and other unknown animals.

Many films have been made that feature real and imaginary monstrous creatures. Some good ones to watch are Alfred Hitchcock's movie, *Birds* and Steven Spielberg's *Jurassic Park*.

There is plenty of information on the Internet as well. A great website devoted to all kinds of fantastic creatures, both past and present is: http://www.syntac.net/hoax/cryptozoo The International Society of Cryptozoology homepage can be found at: http://www.izoo.org/isc

The companion to this book in the Phenomena series is *The Last Dinosaur*. It tells the story of a girl who is searching for her father—as well as the last dinosaur—in the African jungle. Read it yourself and find out where fact meets fiction.

Andrew's note

I've been a big fan of myths and legends all my life. Perhaps I never quite grew up. I enjoy reading about dragons and giants and snake-haired monsters. That's one of the reasons I write fantasy and science fiction stories. This lets me create as many wild and fantastic creatures as I like.

It's almost as much fun trying to discover the truth behind these tales. Sometimes, how a story came about is more intriguing than the story itself.

So, does the Loch Ness monster really exist? Personally, I doubt it. Just as I find it hard to believe that 500,000-year-old ape-men are still roaming the Himalayan Mountains. But that doesn't make them less fascinating. A real Big Foot probably wouldn't be half as interesting as the one created by people's imaginations.

This book only scratches the surface. There is a whole world of creatures for you to explore. Some are only imaginary. Others vanished from the earth long ago. Many are still alive. But they all have one thing in common—they *are* fantastic!

The *Ankylosaurus* had a tail with a heavy knob of bone at the end which could be used to batter an attacker.

Index

Abominable
  Snowman 65–66
Aepyornis maximus
  77–79
Argus 26
Atlas Mountains 13
Australia 79–82

basilisk 24
bestiary 44
Big Foot 54, 66–67

centaur 25
Cerberus 26
Charlemagne 15–16
chimaera 24
coelacanth 54–55
cryptozoology 53, 61,
  66, 67, 69–70
Cyclops 12, 14

dodo 85–86
Dromornis 81
dugong 39–40

Echidna 25, 26
endangered animals
  86–88

faun 25
Feejee Mermaid
  38–39
film monsters 28–29
fossils 13–14

genetic engineering
  30–31, 84–85
Geryon 26
giant 7–10, 14–17
Giant's Causeway 13
Gigantopithecus 66–67
Godzilla 29

Goliath 15
Gorgon 22–23
gorilla 58
griffin 23–24

harpy 23
Hercules 46
hippogriff 23
hoaxes 38–39, 67–69
Hudson, Henry 37
Hydra 46–47

Jersey Devil 53

kakapo 76
kangaroo 80
King Kong 28
kiwi 75, 77
Knossos, Palace of 48
komodo dragon
  58–59

lake monsters 60–61
Lamb of Tartary 27
Loch Ness monster
  54, 59–63
Lovecraft, H.P. 22

mammoth 82–85
manatee 39–40
manticore 25–26
Megamouth 57
mermaid 37–40
Minotaur 47–48
moa 75, 76
Mokele-Mbembe
  63–64

New Zealand 75–77
Nguoi Rung 66

octopus 47

O'Neal, Shaquille 8
oryx, Arabian 45

panda, giant 59
Paul Bunyan 16–17
platypus 80–81
Pyramid, Great 12

rainforest 56
rhinoceros
  black 88
  white 45
  woolly 14

ruhk 78

sasquatch 66
satyr 25
sea monsters 41–42
sphinx 25
spindlehorn 58
squid, giant 42–43
Stonehenge 12

Tree Goose 27–28
Typhon 26

UFO 49
unicorn 44–46

Venezuela 56

Wadlow, Robert 8,
  9–10

yeren 66
Yowie 66